Freedom Fighters

Fannie Lou Hamer

Mark Falstein

Globe Fearon Educational Publisher
Paramus, New Jersey

Paramount Publishing

Freedom Fighters
Cesar Chavez
Fannie Lou Hamer
Martin Luther King, Jr.
Malcolm X
Nelson Mandela

Editor: Tony Napoli
Production editor: Joe C. Shines
Cover and text design: London Road Design
Production: ExecuStaff

Photographs: Cover, pp. 48, 54, 65—UPI/Bettmann Newsphotos; pg. 21—The Bettmann Archive; pp. 38, 57—AP/Wide World Photos

Copyright © 1994 by Globe Fearon Educational Publisher, a division of Paramount Publishing, 240 Frisch Court, Paramus, New Jersey 07652. All rights reserved. No part of this book may be reproduced or transmitted in any form or by any means, electrical or mechanical, including photocopying, recording, or by any information storage and retrieval system, without permission in writing from the publisher.

ISBN 0-8224-3222-6

Printed in the United States of America

4. 10 9 8 7 6 5 4 3 2
MA

Contents

1. The Freedom Riders Come to Sunflower County ... 1
2. "No Colored People Voting in Mississippi" 9
3. "I Ain't Scared of Your Jail" 17
4. Bitter Winter, Freedom Summer 27
5. To Atlantic City 36
6. "I Question America" 44
7. Unbreakable 51
8. To Africa . . . and Back Home 59

CHAPTER 1
The Freedom Riders Come to Sunflower County

The two young men were strangers. Mary Tucker saw that right away. They were too well dressed. Most black folks in Sunflower County, Mississippi, were dirt-poor. Those who had a little money weren't foolish enough to call attention to themselves by their clothes. These young men did not look like fools. They seemed very sure of themselves. They were going from house to house along the dusty, unpaved street, talking to people on their front porches. Mary Tucker could see how scared her neighbors looked. They were shaking their heads at the two men and ducking back inside their houses. She knew who the strangers had to be before the two men reached her house.

"They're freedom riders!" she told herself. "Freedom riders come here at last!"

The year was 1962. Nearly 100 years after the end of slavery, freedom for most African Americans was a hollow word. No part of the United States was completely free of racism. In the South, however, racism was more than a hateful and oppressive attitude. State and local laws ordered *segregation*, or separation of the races. African Americans were barred from most hotels, parks, and restaurants. They were given second-class treatment on buses and trains. Most black people could only get jobs that white people would not take. Those blacks who did the same work as whites usually were paid less.

Black people received second-rate medical care and third-rate education in segregated hospitals and schools. In some counties, no hospital would admit blacks. In others, there was no African American high school. Black people were reminded in dozens of ways that they were not full citizens. They had to step aside when a white person was passing. They had to call whites "sir" and "ma'am." Whites could address them by any insulting name they wished.

Now, however, black people were joining together to demand equality. A movement for civil rights was rolling across the South. Lawyers were using the courts to fight for equal education. Students were sitting down at "whites-only" lunch counters, demanding equal access to public accommodations. People were boycotting businesses that would not hire blacks or that refused equal service to black customers.

In 1961, groups of blacks and whites had challenged segregation laws by riding buses together across the South. People had called them "freedom riders." The name had caught the imagination of Mary Tucker and her neighbors. They called all civil rights workers "freedom riders," no matter what their goals or strategies were.

"Evening, ma'am," one of the young men said to Mrs. Tucker. "We're with the Student Nonviolent Coordinating Committee, and we're talking to people about registering to vote. We're having a mass meeting Monday evening at Williams Chapel Church. Will you come?"

Mrs. Tucker decided at once. She was nearly 70 years old, and she had never voted in her life. However, she would go to this meeting. As the two men talked, she thought of a friend who lived outside of town. "I believe I'll go out in the country and get Fannie Lou," she thought. "I want her to come and hear this. I believe it would mean something to her."

Mrs. Tucker told her friend Fannie Lou about the purpose of the meeting. She said the people there would teach them how to register to vote so they could become full citizens.

Fannie Lou Hamer wanted no part of it. "What for, Tuck?" she snapped. "They taught us that mess in school, and it has turned me off like that." She had been working hard all day and had no time for such nonsense. Black people voting? This was Mississippi.

Then Mrs. Hamer felt sorry for having spoken rudely to her friend. The next evening, she came to Mrs. Tucker's house and apologized. On Monday, she showed up at the meeting despite her feelings about it.

The organizers called it a mass meeting, but the crowd was small. The freedom riders couldn't post notices for their meetings because white people might break them up. About the only place that blacks could meet without making whites nervous was in church. This had been the case since the days of slavery.

The first speaker was a preacher, James Bevel of the Southern Christian Leadership Conference. The SCLC was headed by the most famous freedom rider of all, Dr. Martin Luther King, Jr. The Reverend Bevel talked about Jesus, but he chose a gospel text about "changing times." He tied it in with the idea of registering to vote.

Then James Forman spoke. He was a leader of the Student Nonviolent Coordinating Committee. SNCC, or "snick" as it was called, was largely made up of college students. They challenged segregation laws by simply refusing to obey them. They also organized black people to work for change in their own communities.

The surest way to create change, Forman said, is through the vote. That's why the white man does not want the black man to have it. Voting is *power*. Nearly half of the people of Mississippi are black. In this part of the state, blacks outnumber the whites. However, blacks never have had a chance to elect the people who run their county. If black people were registered, they would have some control over the people who ruled their lives.

This made sense to Mrs. Hamer. She thought of the night police officer in Ruleville. He would go out of his way to brutalize and humiliate black people. If we could vote, she thought, we would have some say over people like that.

Finally, a man named Bob Moses spoke. "Who will come down to the courthouse with me on Friday and try to become a registered voter?" he asked.

Fannie Lou Hamer raised her hand.

Fannie Lou Hamer was born on October 6, 1917, in Montgomery County, Mississippi. Her parents, Jim and Ella Townsend, had 20 children. Fannie Lou was the youngest. When she was two years old, her family moved to a cotton plantation in Sunflower County. They lived in a wooden shack without electricity or running water. Their beds were sacks filled with straw.

Fannie Lou went to work picking cotton when she was six years old. She dropped out of school in the sixth grade to help her family. By the time she was 13, she could pick nearly 300 pounds of cotton per week.

The Townsends owned no land. Like many poor southerners, black and white, they were *sharecroppers*.

The cotton they picked belonged to the white man who owned the plantation. They were allowed to keep and sell a share of it. Every spring, the owner lent them money for seed, food, clothing, and tools. Most sharecroppers had no easy way of getting into town. They had to buy these things at a plantation store. It charged higher prices than the stores in town. Instead of earning money, sharecroppers often ended up owing the landowner after the crop was in.

Fanny Lou was a smart girl. She loved to read. She would read anything she could get her hands on. Often, all she could get were old newspaper and magazine pages that she found by the road. Fannie Lou was good at math, too. She realized that her family was being cheated. One year, she figured that her father was owed $4,000. He was given $200. She knew that if he complained, the entire family would be put off the land.

One year, the family was able to get ahead. Jim Townsend was able to rent land instead of sharecropping. That way he could keep more of the crop for himself. He bought mules, cows, and tools.

The family began to do pretty well. Her father was able to improve their house and even buy a car. One night, however, someone came to their house and put poison in the animal feed. The mules and cows died. A white man had done it—just to put the family back in its "place."

The Townsends worked hard to put food on the table. They would gather cotton scraps after the harvest, walking barefoot in the frozen fields. When they had enough cotton for a bale, they would sell it. Mrs. Townsend would go from farm to farm, helping to kill hogs. As her pay, she took home the guts and feet for her family.

Fannie Lou's life did not change very much even after she had grown up. Her brothers and sisters left Mississippi for new lives in Chicago and other northern cities. Fannie Lou married a sharecropper, Perry Hamer. They settled down on a cotton plantation near Ruleville. By 1962, she had become the timekeeper on the plantation. Other sharecroppers respected her willingness to help people. They also admired her singing. She was a deeply religious woman who knew the Bible better than many preachers. She had grown up singing the music of the southern African American church. Music had always been a way for her to deal with fear and pain. Her rich, low voice was well known in the churches of Sunflower County.

The Hamers had two adopted daughters, Dorothy Jean and Vergie. Mrs. Hamer had become pregnant twice, but both babies were born dead. She still hoped to have children of her own. In 1961, she went into the hospital to have a small tumor removed—"a knot on my stomach," she called it. Later, she learned that she had been sterilized. It had been done without her knowledge or permission. Now she would never be able to have children. She knew that this was often done to poor, rural black women, but there was nothing she could do about it.

There was no thought of taking the doctor to court. She would have to hire a white lawyer. She knew that, even if she could get the money to hire one, no white lawyer would take a case like hers against a white doctor. A year later, when the freedom riders came to Ruleville, she believed that she had one more score to settle with the state of Mississippi.

Fannie Lou was one of 18 people who raised their hands at the meeting that night. "I guess if I had any sense, I would have been a little scared," she later said. "But what was the point of being scared? The only thing they could do to me was kill me. And it seemed like they'd been trying to do that a little bit at a time ever since I could remember."

No one in the church that evening could have imagined that in two years, Fannie Lou Hamer would be challenging the president of the United States.

CHAPTER 2
"No Colored People Voting in Mississippi"

There was a grim joke going around the country during that summer of 1962. A white man and a black man in Mississippi went to register to vote. They were told they had to pass a literacy test. "If you can't read, you can't vote" a county official said. The white man was asked to read a paragraph from the town newspaper. "All right, you pass. You can vote," the official told him. The black man was asked to read from a Chinese newspaper. As he stared at it, the white folks at the courthouse were elbowing each other and grinning.

"What's the problem, boy, can't you read it?" the official said.

"Sure, I can read it," the black man said.

The official laughed. "Then what does it say?"

"It says, 'There ain't gonna be no colored people voting in Mississippi.'"

That joke was not far from the truth. In 1870, Congress passed the 15th Amendment to the Constitution. It gave the freed slaves the right to vote. During the Reconstruction period after the Civil War, many southern blacks were elected to county and state offices. A few were elected to Congress. However, by 1900, whites had gained complete control of most state governments in the South. Literacy tests were one way by which they denied African Americans the vote. In Mississippi, a voter had to explain a section of the state constitution in order to register. A white person would be given a simple section to explain. A black person would be given a section that might confuse even a lawyer.

There were other such tricks. African American people who were trying to register would be told that it was the wrong day or that they had come to the wrong place. They had to fill out a long form. It might be thrown out for any simple mistake. Even a perfect form might get "lost" before election day. In most southern states, people had to pay a poll tax before they could vote. Poor African Americans could not afford the tax. Poor whites were rarely asked to pay it.

The federal government did nothing to stop such actions. The courts said that voting rules were a state matter. Members of Congress from southern states blocked any bill that might change things. James

Eastland, a U.S. senator from Mississippi, was chairman of the Senate Judiciary Committee at this time. He had the power to block the appointment of any federal judge. Eastland owned a 3,800-acre plantation in Sunflower County. He often boasted of how he advanced the cause of white supremacy in Congress.

Fear was a factor, too. Fear was a *large* factor. Black people who voted in Mississippi risked losing their jobs. Those who were brave enough to demand their rights faced violence. They might be dragged from their homes and beaten by hooded terrorists of the Ku Klux Klan. They might have their windows shot out or their houses burned. Beyond that, there was always the threat of lynching. Over the years, there had been many horrible incidents of blacks being killed by white mobs for defying the "southern way of life." In 1955, a 13-year-old Chicago boy named Emmett Till was visiting his cousins near Sunflower County. He was found tortured to death, his body dumped in a pond. His "crime" was insulting a white woman. His killers were never punished.

The people who organized the registration drive in Mississippi knew what they were up against. They knew that the state was a stronghold of racist attitudes. Sunflower County in particular had a reputation for violence against blacks. For this reason and others, fewer than one percent of voting-age blacks in the county were registered.

Bob Moses, a quiet young math teacher from New York, had been signing up voters in Mississippi for a year. He had been beaten and arrested again and again. A local man who worked with him had been murdered. However, Moses had put together a dedicated staff. They came from SNCC and other groups. They worked together as the Council of Federated Organizations. COFO workers went from door to door, asking people to register. They also tried to identify community leaders whom the people trusted. COFO members hoped to train the community leaders to take over the struggle after the members had left the county.

Charles McLaurin was SNCC's 20-year-old field secretary for Sunflower County. Throughout the month of August, his group had been holding meetings. Only three elderly women had been willing to go to the county courthouse in Indianola to try to register. On the morning of August 31, McLaurin was surprised to see 18 people from Ruleville ready to go. A man named Amzie Moore had helped them rent a bus. He was a postal worker from a nearby county who was working closely with COFO.

When the bus arrived at the courthouse, it was met by a crowd of gun-carrying white men. Most of the Ruleville people were not sure what to do. Fannie Lou Hamer stepped off the bus and walked up the courthouse steps. The others followed. They were given the usual literacy test, the usual forms to fill out, the usual runaround. None of the 18 was allowed to register.

As the bus headed back to Ruleville, it was stopped by a police car. The bus driver was arrested. According to the police officer, the bus was "too yellow." It looked like a school bus. The driver was taken back to Indianola. Hours ticked away as the bus sat by the side of the road. The passengers began talking in worried tones. Suddenly, breaking through their growing fear, came the strong, low voice of a woman singing hymns. Her singing seemed to calm the other riders.

"Who is that woman?" Charles McLaurin asked.

"That's Mrs. Hamer," several people told him. "Fannie Lou Hamer."

It was evening by the time that Mrs. Hamer got home. Her family had some troubling news. The plantation owner, Mr. W. D. Marlow, had confronted them that day. He knew that Mrs. Hamer had gone to register. He had threatened to kick her off the plantation.

Minutes later, Marlow drove up. He asked her if it was true that she had been to Indianola to try to register. Fannie Lou didn't hesitate with her answer.

"Yes, sir, Mr. Marlow, I sure did," she replied.

"Well, if you want to stay here and everything go like it always is, you better go back down there and get your name off that book," he said.

"I didn't go down there to register for you," Fannie Lou Hamer told her boss. "I went down to register for myself."

When Marlow was gone, the Hamers talked things over. "Pap" Hamer had to stay on the plantation until the crop was in, or their family would have nothing to eat that winter. However, he knew it wasn't safe for his wife to be there—not after talking that way to a white man. Fannie's husband helped her pack and drove her and their daughters to Ruleville. Fannie Lou went straight to a voter-registration meeting and told everyone what had happened.

The SNCC workers were shocked. They were all young college students. Here was a woman with a family, without much education, who had given up her job—and her home—for freedom.

Mary Tucker offered to let Fannie Lou stay in her house. The next day, Marlow sent word that she could come home. He didn't want to put her off the plantation where she had lived and worked for 18 years. He was just mad about all of the people coming on his land and talking about voting. If Fannie Lou came back, he said, "things would be like they always were."

"That's what I'm trying to get out of," she replied. "Things being like they always was. I want some change."

Mrs. Hamer decided to stay with her friends in Ruleville for a few days. Then her husband became afraid that someone might try to kill her. He took her to stay with relatives in another county.

Several days passed. One rainy evening, there was a knock on the door of the cabin where she was staying. A young black man stood in a shadow on the doorstep. "I'm looking for Fannie Lou Hamer," he said.

"I'm Fannie Lou Hamer," she said.

"Do you remember me?" the young man said. "I'm Charles McLaurin. From the bus to Indianola?"

Fannie Lou remembered.

"Mrs. Hamer, Bob Moses asked me to 'go find that lady who was kicked off her plantation and who sang all those church songs on the bus.' We would like you to tell your story at a SNCC conference in Nashville, Tennessee."

Fannie Lou Hamer didn't hesitate. "I'll be ready in a minute," she said.

For Mrs. Hamer, a door had opened. She had read about the freedom rides and protest marches. She had wanted to get involved in the civil rights movement herself but had not known how to join. Wherever the movement was, there was no sign of it in Ruleville, Mississippi. Now it had come to her.

Amzie Moore had put the SNCC workers in touch with Mrs. Hamer. For McLaurin and Moses, she was just the type of grass-roots leader that the movement needed. SNCC was having no success in winning over the "leaders" of the local African American community. These ministers and teachers were afraid to challenge the system. Many of the local people hated them for it.

Now here was a poor sharecropper, a representative of the people whose lives they were trying to change. She shared the people's fears, yet she had overcome them. She was smart, she was respected, and she had an amazing presence. She had decided that she wasn't going to let anyone turn her around. She could inspire others to make the same decision.

That night, McLaurin and Mrs. Hamer drove to Tougaloo College, a black school near Jackson, the state capital. At the college, they met up with other SNCC members. They drove in a convoy to Nashville. When Fannie Lou spoke to the Nashville group, her story moved the SNCC leadership just as it had the students in Ruleville. When she led the meeting in song, she seemed to inspire everyone with courage.

Some of the students had formed a group called the SNCC Freedom Singers. They gave concerts to raise money for the movement's activities. They were about to go on a tour. They asked Mrs. Hamer if she would join them. It would be several months before she returned home.

CHAPTER 3
"I Ain't Scared of Your Jail"

Ten days after Fannie Lou Hamer tried to register to vote, gunshots were fired into Mary Tucker's house. They slammed into the wall above the bed where Mrs. Hamer had been sleeping. Shots were fired into Joe and Rebecca McDonald's house, too. They had put up several of the SNCC workers. Shots were also fired into the home of Herman Sisson, who was active in the registration drive. His 20-year-old granddaughter and her friend were wounded.

The shootings halted the registration drive. People were afraid to be seen with SNCC workers or to invite them into their homes. The students had experienced this before in other places. They knew that they had to win back the people's trust. They did not want anyone to think that they would come in, stir up trouble for the local people, and leave. Instead of pushing people to register, they helped out in the community. They did chores. They gave farm people rides into town to shop. They helped sharecroppers get the government food that many of them needed to make it through the winter when there was no farm work.

Among these people that the SNCC workers helped were Pap Hamer and his daughters. They had left the Marlow plantation and moved into town. Most black people in Ruleville wanted nothing to do with the Hamers. Fannie Lou's action had scared them. The Reverend Bevel had to get $50 from the SCLC to move the Hamers' furniture into town. In most years, Pap Hamer was able to find a winter job. This year, nobody would give him work.

Fannie Lou had returned to Ruleville in November, but she could not return to her old life. The SNCC tour had set her on a new path. The attention she got wherever she told her story made her aware of a power she never knew she had.

In December, Mrs. Hamer went back to Indianola to take the voter-registration test again. SNCC workers had been helping her study the Mississippi state constitution. She thought she had done well. "You had better let me sign up," she told the county official, "because I'm going to keep coming back until you do." In January, she learned that she had passed. The next day, she went to the Ruleville city hall and registered to vote.

After five months, however, the overall registration drive had little success. Many poor blacks had even less schooling than Mrs. Hamer. Quite a few went to work so young that they had never learned to read. They had no idea what citizenship meant or what to expect when they went to register. Many had no idea that they *could* register.

The Southern Christian Leadership Conference was trying to deal with this problem. The SCLC ran a school in Dorchester, Georgia. It trained people to teach reading and citizenship classes. The director of the school was a young minister named Andrew Young. He asked James Bevel to choose a group of Mississippi people to be trained at Dorchester. Fannie Lou Hamer was one of the people he chose.

In April 1963, the Mississippians traveled to Dorchester on a bus. Mrs. Hamer soon became a leader of their group. Young and his assistant, Dorothy Cotton, were impressed by her strength and self-confidence. "She would shine her light on those workshops," Cotton later remembered. Singing was an important part of their meetings, and Fannie Lou had a powerful voice. They sang hymns, old slave songs of the Underground Railroad, and new "freedom songs," such as "We Shall Overcome" and "I Ain't Scared of Your Jail."

Later that spring, Mrs. Hamer was chosen to go to Charleston, South Carolina, for more training. When the course was finished, the Mississippians boarded a bus for home. Among the group was Annell Ponder, an SCLC staff member who was a teacher at a black college in Greenwood, Mississippi. Two of the women, Euvester Simpson and June Johnson, were still in their teens. Johnson, only 15, had defied her mother to work in the civil rights movement. Her mother was afraid for her safety. She gave June permission to go to Charleston only after she learned that the well-respected Ponder would be going.

The group was full of confidence as they traveled across the South. In Charleston, Mrs. Hamer had visited the Old Slave Mart. She saw the pen in which her people had been chained like animals. She saw the stump from which they had been sold as property. It made her more determined than ever to help them cast off the chains that still held them.

When the bus stopped in Columbus, Mississippi, the group sat down at a whites-only lunch counter in the bus station. They were stared at, and remarks were made, but they were served. Then, when they were in line to get back on the bus, the driver pushed a little white girl ahead of them. "No niggers at the front of the line," he ordered.

Fannie Lou was furious. She demanded the bus driver's name and number. She insisted that she was going to do something about the way they had been treated. As the bus rolled across Mississippi, the group

For decades in the south, blacks were forced to use separate facilities in everything from public transportation to public drinking fountains.

sang freedom songs. Meanwhile, the driver got out and made a phone call at every stop.

When the bus reached Winona, the next large town, the police were waiting. Some of the group sat down at the counter in the café to order lunch. An officer tapped Annell Ponder on the shoulder with a billy club. He ordered her to leave. When she protested that his action was against the law, he said, "Ain't no damn law, you just get out of here!" Euvester Simpson tried to use the rest room. She was told to go to the one for "colored."

When Ponder started writing down the number of the police car, the chief of police placed the group under arrest. He ordered them into the car.

At this point, Mrs. Hamer stepped off the bus. She asked the others if they wanted her to go on without them. "Get that one there!" the police chief ordered, pointing at her. "Get that one there—bring her down in the other car!"

Five women and one man were brought to the county jail. It was Sunday, June 9, 1963.

Later, in court, police officers would swear that the prisoners' injuries resulted from their falling down or being dragged across the floor after they refused to go to their cells. The prisoners, however, told a different story.

Because of her age, June Johnson wasn't put in a cell at first. The officers beat her, she later testified, after she protested that the police "were supposed to protect people." Then they threw her into jail with the others.

Annell Ponder was beaten by "at least three" officers. They kept trying to get her to call them "sir," and she refused. She testified that they kept hitting her "with blackjacks, fists, open palm."

James West, the only man in the group, was taken to a cell called "the bullpen." The police brought in some of the jail inmates. According to one who later testified in court, the police chief and the sheriff ordered them to take turns beating West with a blackjack. Then West was carried out. Fannie Lou Hamer was brought in.

One of the officers had called Ruleville. He had learned of Mrs. Hamer's role in the voter-registration movement. The officers insulted her and cursed her. "You went [to Charleston] to see Martin Luther King," one of them said. "We're not going to have it." An officer ordered a black inmate to beat her. He warned the inmate that if he refused to use the blackjack on her, "You know what I'll use on you."

Mrs. Hamer couldn't believe that a black man would do this to her. The inmate ordered her to lie on a bed with her face down, and he beat her until he was tired. Then a second inmate took his turn. The beating stopped only after Mrs. Hamer agreed to sign a statement that she had been treated well.

That night, Euvester Simpson stayed up nursing Mrs. Hamer. Fannie Lou was in good spirits despite her beating. However, her legs and back were bruised and bleeding. It would be weeks before she could lie on her back again.

Early Monday morning, the six blacks were taken to court. There was no lawyer to represent them. There was no trial. All of them except June Johnson were fined $100. Then they were returned to jail.

Meanwhile, people at the SNCC office in Greenwood knew that something was wrong when the six workers didn't check in. The SNCC office called the police in Winona. "We know you're holding our people," they said. "We know you mean to kill them. We've called the

FBI." This was a bluff. Nobody at SNCC knew where the six were being held. They were making the same call to all of the towns along the bus route.

At last, SNCC learned of the arrests from other people who had been on the bus. Two SNCC workers went to Winona to investigate. One of them, Lawrence Guyot, was arrested for "disturbing the peace." The police beat him after he refused to call an officer "sir." They tried to get him to sign a paper saying that he had been arrested for drunk driving and had fallen out of the car. Guyot refused; he didn't even know how to drive. The police placed a knife within reach of his cell. Guyot was certain that they were planning to trap him into trying to escape so that they could shoot him.

By then, the police were getting calls from all over the country. SNCC had alerted the press. Eleanor Holmes Norton, a law student working for SNCC for the summer, went to Winona to try to get the prisoners freed. She had no money for bail and was refused. It was not until June 12, when Andrew Young, Dorothy Cotton, and James Bevel arrived, that the prisoners were released.

The civil rights movement was dominating the news that month. In Alabama, Governor George Wallace blocked a door at the state university to prevent African American students from enrolling. In Jackson, Mississippi, black leader Medgar Evers was murdered in front of his own home. Finally the federal government was beginning to take notice—and to act. President John F.

Kennedy spoke to the nation on television. He sent a far-reaching new civil rights law to Congress. If it passed, it would make all segregation illegal.

With these other events making news, the Winona incident did not get much public notice. However the federal government was paying attention. Attorney General Robert Kennedy, the president's brother, took an interest in the case. The FBI questioned Mrs. Hamer and the others. On June 17, the U.S. government sued the city of Winona. In September, charges were filed against the police chief, the sheriff, and other officers. They were accused of brutally beating the prisoners and forcing them to sign statements against their will.

The trial was held in Oxford, Mississippi. It began on December 2. The case came down to a simple question: What had happened at the jail in Winona? Fannie Lou Hamer and the others testified that they had been beaten. One of the black inmates who had been forced to beat them supported their story. Doctors testified that their injuries could only have been caused by beating.

The officers on trial testified that no beatings had taken place. They claimed that the prisoners had been injured because they "kicked and fought." The officers' lawyers kept repeating that the prisoners were civil rights workers. They called them "professional agitators" whose actions had been intended to cause trouble.

The outcome of the trial was never in doubt. The victims were black. The police officers were white. The jury members all were white. It took them little time to find the officers not guilty.

Again, the press paid little attention. The trial took place only days after President Kennedy was assassinated in Dallas, Texas. Newspapers around the country were filled with stories about the shocking murder of the young president and then the murder of his accused assassin. Throughout the civil rights movement, however, word was beginning to spread about Fannie Lou Hamer.

CHAPTER 4
Bitter Winter, Freedom Summer

By the fall of 1963, the SNCC-led voter-registration drive had been going on for two years. But SNCC workers were discouraged. It seemed that they had made almost no progress. Few people had tried to register. Many of those who did had lost their jobs. In August, Mrs. Hamer had gone proudly to the town hall to vote in an election for state governor. She was turned away for not having paid her poll tax for the past two years. Of course she hadn't paid the tax—she hadn't been registered.

Few people outside of Mississippi seemed to know or care about these problems. The federal government did nothing to change things. White liberals sent money to support other civil rights efforts. However, they seemed to regard voting rights in Mississippi as a hopeless cause. The feeling, even among many civil rights supporters, seemed to be that Mississippi's blacks didn't care about voting.

COFO wanted to prove that they did care. They held a mock election. Aaron Henry, a black drugstore owner, was the "freedom candidate" for governor. Ed King, a white professor at Tougaloo College, was the candidate for lieutenant governor. They called for an end to segregation and a cutoff of tax money to racist organizations. They also called for more black police officers, more money for public schools, aid to poor farmers, and a law against threatening voters.

Whites were invited to vote in the mock election, but a special effort was made to reach blacks. More than 100 white students from Yale and Stanford universities came to Mississippi. They drove up and down the state's back roads. They talked to people in rural counties and helped them get to the voting places.

More than 80,000 people voted in the mock election. It proved that Mississippi blacks *would* vote if they could only register. Now COFO targeted 1964, a presidential election year, for an all-out registration drive.

Some SNCC workers wanted to bring in more white students to sign up voters. They felt that the whites had been helpful in the earlier efforts. They also thought that if whites were involved, maybe people in power would pay attention. Maybe the federal government would provide some protection.

Other SNCC workers were against the idea. They claimed that the SNCC was building a grass-roots organization. They were training their own people to change their lives. It had not been easy getting the blacks in Mississippi to realize that they could do it themselves. Some black activists were afraid that the local blacks would start looking to the white outsiders for leadership. Then, they asked, what would happen after the whites left?

Fannie Lou Hamer helped decide the question. "If we're trying to break down this barrier of segregation, we can't segregate ourselves," she said. And so, Freedom Summer was launched.

A call went out for white volunteers. COFO screened the volunteers and chose 1,000 to come to Mississippi. COFO announced its plans to the federal government and the press. It would hold an information campaign to show the nation how black people lived in Mississippi.

To begin the campaign, SNCC held a leadership conference in Washington, D.C. African American leaders from across the country were there. James Forman and Bob Moses made speeches. They hinted about the contradictions that they hoped to show that summer between what was going on in Mississippi and United States law. The great African American writer, James Baldwin, made a speech. People from government agencies gave talks on health care, education, and legal rights.

The conference, however, was turning into a bore. The press was giving it little notice. People were talking during the speeches. The SNCC leaders were discouraged. Then someone suggested that Fannie Lou Hamer be called up to speak.

Most people at the conference knew of Mrs. Hamer, but few had ever heard her speak. As she began to talk about her life as a sharecropper, silence settled over the hall. She told about what had happened when she tried to register to vote. She described what had happened to her in Winona. She spoke of what blacks and poor whites needed to do to win their fair share of the American dream.

The people at the conference were awed. They had rarely heard anyone speak with such force. It was not a prepared speech, but a talk straight from the heart. What Fannie Lou was saying about freedom and justice captured in simple language what everyone felt. It didn't matter that this woman had little education. Here was the spirit of the civil rights movement standing before them.

Fannie Lou closed by singing her favorite hymn, "This Little Light of Mine." It seemed to sum up exactly what SNCC was trying to do in Mississippi. She was just a "little light," one human soul, but she had made a difference. Every little light could make a difference.

SNCC leaders wanted to make use of Mrs. Hamer's amazing ability to reach people. Attorney General Robert Kennedy was the person that they particularly wanted to reach. If Freedom Summer was to succeed, they believed, federal officers must be sent to Mississippi. Otherwise, the violence would be terrible. The new president, Lyndon Johnson, said that he supported civil rights. However, SNCC doubted whether he, a southerner, was eager to confront white Mississippi. Robert Kennedy, on the other hand, might listen. He was the key to getting Johnson to act. What was the best way to approach the attorney general? SNCC thought that it might be through Cardinal Richard Cushing. This powerful official of the Roman Catholic Church was a friend of the Kennedy family. In December 1963, SNCC sent Fannie Lou Hamer to Boston to speak to him.

The meeting went badly. Mrs. Hamer was not her usual confident self. She was nervous. She wasn't sure how she, a Protestant, should talk to a cardinal. She was worried that she might embarrass herself. She did not state clearly what she wanted. The cardinal would not be of any help to the movement.

Mrs. Hamer was depressed. She felt that she had let the movement down. Back home in Ruleville, things were desperate. It was winter. Many people had been fired for working in the registration drive. Others had lost their jobs because new farm machinery made many workers unnecessary. Also, a group of white Mississippians was spying on the movement and finding new ways to block its work.

Mrs. Hamer was directing a clothing drive that winter. A group in Boston called Friends of SNCC collected 30,000 pounds of clothing for out-of-work farm workers and their families. It was brought by truck to the Hamers' house. Mrs. Hamer had only one rule about who could receive clothing. They had to go to the courthouse and try to register to vote.

Ruleville's Mayor Dorrough tried to stop the program. He tried to have Mrs. Hamer arrested, but there was no law against giving away clothes. Then he announced on the radio that she was giving away free clothing and food. People should go to her house and "just take it." Some people were angry when they found out about her rule. Despite her efforts, only a handful of blacks had even tried to become registered voters.

African Americans needed to see that there was nothing mysterious about politics. In March 1964, civil rights organizers formed the Mississippi Freedom Democratic Party, or MFDP. They chose this name to show that they had been kept out of the state's regular Democratic Party organization. The MFDP ran candidates for Congress in the Democratic primary. Fannie Lou Hamer was the candidate in the Second District. Victoria Gray, a civil rights worker from Hattiesburg, was the Freedom Democrats' candidate for the U.S. Senate.

Most southern Democrats in 1964 had little in common with the national Democratic Party. In the South, the party stood for states' rights. For some southerners, states' rights meant the right of a state to ignore and oppose federal laws. As one Mississippi politician bluntly put it, "If you say you're for states' rights, that means you're for segregation." However, southern politics was Democratic party politics. In Civil War days, the Republicans had been the antislavery party, and the white southerners had never forgotten. Southern states sometimes voted for a Republican for president. On the state and local level, however, the Democrats were the only party that mattered.

Lawrence Guyot was chosen to be MFDP chair. Fannie Lou Hamer was named vice-chair. Of course, the MFDP knew that their candidates had no hope of winning. They just wanted to show black Mississippians what voting could accomplish. They would show them that they had the same right to run for office as any other American.

Since 1941, the Delta counties of the Second District had been represented in Congress by Jamie Whitten. In her speeches, Mrs. Hamer noted that Whitten had never done anything for even the poorer white people of his district. His policies helped only rich planters. He had voted against government aid for education. Why? Because some of the money would have gone to black schools. He had voted against a program that would have helped poor farm workers learn to use modern farm machinery. Why? Because it would have allowed workers to bargain for higher pay. Fannie Lou promised that, if elected, she would work for all of the people, regardless of race or class.

The primary election turned out as expected. Mrs. Hamer and the other Freedom Democrats lost badly.

However, they were far from through. Long before the election, the MFDP was making plans that would change politics in the South forever.

A few days after the primary, volunteers chosen for Freedom Summer began to gather in Oxford, Ohio. At the same time, COFO announced its plans at a conference in Washington, D.C. The place and time were chosen in the hope of getting government help. Fannie Lou Hamer and others described what happened to black Mississippians who dared to seek first-class citizenship. They told of the beatings, bombings, shootings, and endless harassment. Now white students were coming to help make Mississippi part of America again. Would the government send federal marshals to Mississippi to protect these young men and women? The government would not.

Bob Moses led the training sessions in Ohio. The students learned how to protect themselves when beaten and kicked. They saw films that showed what they could expect in Mississippi. Also, they met Mrs. Hamer, who quickly put them under her spell. She talked, she sang, she taught the well-to-do students about the people with whom they would be working. They must respect the deep religious feelings of black southerners, she told them. They must feel no hate, even for the most racist whites. Hatred had no place in her life, and it should have none in theirs.

In small groups, the students began to head south. Many had not yet left Ohio by June 21, when news came from Neshoba County, Mississippi. Two white volunteers and a local black man had been arrested in the town of Philadelphia. Then they had been taken out of the jail. That was the last time anyone had seen Andrew Goodman, Michael Schwerner, and James Chaney. It was feared that they had been murdered.

On this note, Freedom Summer began.

CHAPTER 5
To Atlantic City

"Invasion!" newspaper headlines screamed. "Outsiders are invading Mississippi to break up our customs and force their ideas on us!" The state government passed more than 20 new laws restricting meetings and free speech. The mayor of Jackson doubled the size of the police force. The city bought 250 shotguns and an armored truck.

"You are not going to Mississippi to try to be heroes," Bob Moses told the volunteers. He warned them to try to stay out of danger—and out of jail, if possible. Their job, he said, was to try to leave behind three people who would be stronger than before the workers arrived. That way, there would be 3,000 more people to push their cause in Mississippi.

Thirty volunteers were based in Ruleville. It was a center for civil rights work. Mrs. Hamer, Mary Tucker, Joe McDonald, and many others brought students into their homes. The Hamers' small house became the local headquarters.

In southern communities, people were not used to seeing blacks and whites walking together, eating together, working together. Mrs. Hamer coached the students on what sort of behavior was safe and what was likely to cause violence. Don't walk down the street hand in hand, she told them. Don't ride around on motorcycles together.

There was an uneasy peace in Mississippi during that summer of 1964. There was wild talk of "communists in our midst" and even a few arrests. In Ruleville, as in other towns, some local whites shouted insults and threw trash at the volunteers. Rocks and bottles were thrown at cars. In the worst incident, the church where SNCC and COFO held their meetings was set on fire. But Pap Hamer phoned in the alarm, and the fire was quickly put out.

Although there was little actual violence, there was great fear. Mrs. Hamer and other blacks received death threats. Police cars followed volunteers around as they tried to sign up voters. Many of the local people were afraid to talk to them. In everyone's mind was a question: What had happened to Chaney, Goodman, and Schwerner? Their burned-out car had been found, but there was still no sign of the three young men. The FBI investigated. They searched the woods and dragged the rivers and the swamps. They

Student volunteers came to Mississippi in the summer of 1964 to help register blacks to vote.

found several bodies and parts of bodies, but not the ones they were looking for.

Somehow, the volunteers' work got done. They got local high-school students involved in voter registration. They set up community centers and "freedom schools." They gave free medical and legal services. They gathered support for the Mississippi Freedom Democratic Party. The MFDP wanted to show blacks how to use the political system. It wanted to build an organization through which the poor could challenge the people in power. This is how Americans have always organized to create change, volunteers said. You've been left out.

The MFDP had a more immediate goal, as well. It wanted to take the place of the state's all-white delegation at the upcoming Democratic National Convention. The Democrats would be meeting in Atlantic City, New Jersey, during the last week of August. Everyone knew that they would nominate Lyndon Johnson for a full term as president. Johnson had pushed Congress to pass President Kennedy's civil rights bill, but civil rights were not political power. That power came from money, votes, and organization. Black Mississippians were poor, and they were not allowed to vote. Now, however, they were organizing.

White Democrats were choosing their delegates to the convention at meetings around the state. African Americans were kept out of the process by the usual tricks. In some towns, blacks were allowed to sit in on the meetings, but they couldn't nominate delegates. They couldn't vote or help count the votes. Very well, the MFDP said. We'll open *our* meetings to anyone who wants to come. We'll follow all of the rules of the national Democratic Party.

The MFDP held its own local, county, and state meetings. It chose its own delegates for Atlantic City. There it planned to issue a challenge to the national convention: Who will be seated as the Mississippi delegation? The all-white group, or "the only democratically [chosen] body of Mississippi citizens worthy of taking part in [the] convention's business"? The all-white delegation hated President Johnson for forcing civil rights on the South. Everyone knew that in November, many of them would support the Republican candidate, Barry Goldwater. The Freedom Democrats would be loyal to their party's nominee. Which group would the convention choose to seat?

The regular Mississippi Democratic Party held its state convention on August 6. Not one black delegate was elected. On that same day, the MFDP held its own state convention. Earlier that week, the bodies of the three missing civil rights workers had been found. All three had been shot. James Chaney had been tortured, as well. As the COFO had bitterly predicted, when white people were killed, Americans took notice. Now maybe they would pay attention to the outrage that was taking place in Mississippi. Now maybe they would do something.

Some people were already doing something. At the MFDP state convention was a man named Joseph Rauh. He was a lawyer for the United Automobile Workers labor union. He was also a Democratic party leader and an active supporter of civil rights. That spring, Rauh had met Bob Moses at a meeting. Moses had asked his opinion of their chance of unseating the regular Mississippi delegation. Rauh thought that they had a good chance. Everyone knew that Johnson would be the nominee. Johnson would choose the vice-president, and his supporters would write the party platform. The convention would be dull. An MFDP challenge might "stir things up."

It would all come down to the credentials committee, of which Rauh was a member. This group of 110 delegates would decide whether each state's delegation had been chosen fairly. If just 11 of them, ten percent, thought that the MFDP had a case, the question would go *to the floor*, before the whole convention. If that happened, northern blacks and white liberals might have the votes to seat the Freedom Democrats.

The MFDP state convention chose 34 delegates and 34 alternates to go to Atlantic City. All but four of them were African Americans. Some were doctors, teachers, and other educated professionals. About half were poor rural people. Aaron Henry, the candidate for governor in the mock election, was chosen to chair the delegation. Fannie Lou Hamer was elected vice-chair. Delegates included Charles McLaurin, Victoria Gray, Lawrence Guyot, and Ed King.

Ella Baker, one of the founders of SNCC, spoke at the state meeting. She talked about the grim discovery in Neshoba County. "The symbol of politics in Mississippi lies in those three bodies that were dug from the earth," she said. Joseph Rauh also spoke. He told the group that he fully expected delegates from such states as New York, California, and Illinois to support the MFDP at the national convention. He thought that as many as two thirds of the 5,000 total delegates in Atlantic City would vote for MFDP's delegation instead of the all-white Democratic group.

However, President Johnson was furious at Rauh for working with the Freedom Democrats. Johnson felt that he was doing more for black Americans than any other president ever had. However, he wanted change to come at his own pace. If the Democrats pushed the race issue now, they could lose in November. He wanted no challenges at "his" convention. He wanted it all to go smoothly.

The president tried to pressure Rauh to drop his support for the MFDP. Senator Hubert Humphrey of Minnesota was one of Rauh's closest friends. Johnson had planned to name Humphrey as his vice-president. Now he threatened to drop him if Rauh didn't drop the MFDP.

Johnson's other "pressure point" against Rauh was Walter Reuther. He was the president of the United Automobile Workers, the union that Rauh worked for. Reuther also wanted Humphrey to be vice-president, and someday perhaps president. Johnson told Reuther that Rauh would be to blame if Humphrey didn't get the job.

None of the MFDP delegates knew about any of this when they headed for Atlantic City.

CHAPTER 6
"I Question America"

Fannie Lou Hamer spent the week before the Democratic Convention traveling up and down the East Coast, rallying support for the MFDP. Then she returned to Mississippi to ride the bus to Atlantic City with the other delegates. The day they arrived, they began talking to delegates from other states. They held rallies on Atlantic City's famous boardwalk. As Rauh had expected, the MFDP challenge was big news. Its rallies were covered by every TV network.

The convention was scheduled to open on Monday, August 24. On the Saturday before, the credentials committee met. The party had given the group a room that was just big enough for the committee members and the witnesses. There was no room for TV cameras. One newsperson alerted Rauh to this plan. Together they made sure that cameras were squeezed in.

Rauh had one hour to present his case. He had to prove that the MFDP represented the Democratic Party in Mississippi better than the regulars. Aaron Henry and Ed King were his first witnesses. They spoke of the racism and violence that defined life in their state. The committee chairman asked that the witnesses not talk about "the general life of the state of Mississippi." The job of the committee was just to decide whether the regular state delegation had been fairly or unfairly chosen.

Rauh, however, wanted the committee to hear firsthand accounts of the violence that African Americans in Mississippi faced if they tried to register. He believed that it was very important for the committee to understand why blacks were not voting. He also wanted the committee to hear from Fannie Lou Hamer.

Mrs. Hamer took her seat at the witness table. "Mr. Chairman and the credentials committee," she began. "My name is Fannie Lou Hamer. . . . I live at 626 East Lafayette Street, Ruleville, Mississippi, Sunflower County.

"It was the 31st of August in 1962 that 18 of us traveled 26 miles to the county courthouse in Indianola to try to register to become first-class citizens. . . ."

Fannie Lou talked and talked, as if someone had wound her up. She told the story that was so familiar to people in Mississippi but that most of the country was hearing for the first time. She described what happened when she went to register and how she was put off the plantation. She talked about the shootings in Ruleville. She told about the arrests in Winona.

"I was carried to the county jail and . . placed in a cell. . . . After I was placed in the cell, I began to hear . . . the sounds of licks and horrible screams. And I could hear somebody say, 'Can you say "yes sir," nigger? Can you say "yes, sir?" ' And they would say other horrible names.

"It wasn't too long before three white men came to my cell. One of them asked me where I was from, and I told him Ruleville. He said, 'We are going to check this.' And they left my cell, and it wasn't too long before they came back. He said, 'You are from Ruleville, all right,' and he used a curse word, and he said, 'We are going to make you wish you were dead.' "

Tears welled up in Fannie Lou's eyes as she told of her own beating. There were tears in the eyes of some of the country's leading politicians, too.

"All of this is on account we want to register, to become first-class citizens," she went on. "And if the Freedom Democratic Party is not seated now, I question America. Is this America, the land of the free and the home of the brave? Is this where we have to sleep with our telephones off the hooks because our lives are threatened daily because we want to live as decent human beings, in America?

"Thank you."

Other witnesses followed. Rita Schwerner, the widow of the murdered Michael Schwerner, spoke for the MFDP. Martin Luther King urged the committee to support the Freedom Democrats.

Then the regular Mississippi Democrats had their turn. They tried to argue that the MFDP didn't represent anyone. They claimed that no one was kept out of the political process in their state. They labeled Fannie Lou's story "pitiful." They pointed out that when Fannie Lou had run for Congress, she didn't even get the votes of the majority of registered Negro voters in her district. As for party loyalty, not one of the regulars would promise to support the party's nominee in November.

Afterward, Mrs. Hamer learned that her full story hadn't been seen on television that afternoon. The president had called a news conference, and it was covered by all of the major TV networks. That evening, however, her testimony was run and rerun on every network. It turned out to be the biggest news story of the day.

Mrs. Hamer was interviewed for the Sunday *New York Times.* The reporter asked her why she didn't just leave Mississippi for the North, as so many other blacks had done. "Why should I leave Mississippi?" she replied. "I go to the big city, and with the kind of education they give us in Mississippi . . . I'd wind up [on welfare]. That's why I want to change things in Mississippi. You don't run away from problems—you just face them."

Fannie Lou Hamer walks toward the convention hall entrance at Atlantic City, New Jersey. Three days earlier she gained national attention with her testimony before the Democratic convention's credentials committee.

Phone calls poured in to the White House and the convention delegates. Democrats around the country were urging their leaders to support the MFDP!

The leaders had other ideas. The party was under pressure from southern delegates. A credentials committee hearing was one thing. A debate on the floor of the convention was another. It would embarrass the South. It would cost the Democrats southern votes. If a "white backlash" spread to other parts of the country, it might even cost Johnson the election.

Northern white liberals were worried. Even black delegates were uncomfortable. It was important for Johnson to win in November. He would be far better for civil rights than Barry Goldwater. Yet how would it look on national TV if liberals and blacks voted to seat the all-white delegation? The matter could not be allowed to reach the floor of the convention. It had to be settled before the credentials committee made its report on Tuesday.

The committee named a subcommittee of eight to work out a compromise. It was headed by Walter Mondale, who would later become a senator from Minnesota and vice president of the United States. For three days, the group argued about different ideas. One idea, Mondale later said, "was you just take the black delegation and . . . kick the white delegation out." But Mondale knew that this solution would not solve any long-term problems. There would be no hope of both whites and blacks existing peaceably together in the Democratic party in the South.

Another idea was to seat the MFDP in the balcony as "honored guests." This sounded too much like "the back of the bus." The balcony was where blacks had to sit in Mississippi movie theaters. "We won't settle for that in Atlantic City," Aaron Henry told the MFDP.

Edith Green, congresswoman from Oregon, suggested that anyone from either delegation who would take an oath of loyalty to the party's nominee should be seated.

Even with all of these suggestions, however, everyone knew that there was only one Democrat whose opinion counted. That was the president—Lyndon Johnson—and his mind was made up. He told Hubert Humphrey that if Humphrey wanted to be vice-president, he was going to have to "stop those people from Mississippi."

CHAPTER 7
Unbreakable

On Monday, August 24, hours before the convention opened, Fannie Lou Hamer got a call from Charles Diggs. He was a black congressman from Michigan who was on the credentials committee. Diggs was setting up a meeting with Senator Humphrey, MFDP leaders, and the credentials subcommittee members.

Black people respected Hubert Humphrey. He had been pushing for civil rights since 1948, long before it was popular. If he became vice-president, they knew he would support programs to help black people and the poor. Fannie Lou later told people that she was happy just to have the opportunity to talk to Humphrey. At this meeting, however, that she realized that the MFDP was being pushed aside.

Aaron Henry and Ed King were at the meeting. Joseph Rauh was there. Martin Luther King was there. Seated among them, "with his eyes full of tears," was Senator

Humphrey. He asked them to back off. Don't let your challenge come to the convention floor, he said.

Then Joseph Rauh spoke. He urged the MFDP members to listen to the senator. If they didn't stop pushing, he said, Mr. Humphrey would not be nominated for vice-president. Then there was Dr. King, the movement's most respected leader. He did not try to tell them what to do, but his presence was clearly supposed to persuade them to change their minds.

Mrs. Hamer was amazed—and she was angry. Here was their own lawyer, telling them to give up their fight. Mrs. Hamer could not keep silent. Did the senator believe that his becoming vice-president was more important than the lives of 400,000 black people in Mississippi? she asked. She went on to tell him that she thought he was a good man who knew what was right. But, she added, he was afraid to do what was right. She told Humphrey that if he forced the MFDP to back off just so he could be the vice president, then he would not "be worth anything." Finally, Fannie Lou said that she would pray that he would do the right thing.

The MFDP needed more than prayer. It needed the votes of 11 delegates on the credentials committee, and suddenly its support was vanishing. That evening, as the convention delegates listened to the opening speeches, Joseph Rauh went around the floor. He asked dozens of respected liberals if they would speak for the MFDP. Nobody would. They all agreed that the MFDP should be seated. However, they wouldn't do anything to hurt Humphrey's chances.

The MFDP had demanded a role in the national political arena. The game played in that arena was hardball. Lyndon Johnson was a champion at hardball politics. One MFDP delegate later claimed that Johnson got a black congressman to befriend the group. The MFDP gave the congressman a list of the members of the credentials committee who would support the MFDP. Then, every person on that list received a telephone call. They were told such things as 'Your husband is up for a judgeship, and if you don't shape up, he won't get it,' or 'You're up for a loan, and if you don't shape up, you won't get it.' It didn't take long for the MFDP group to realize the kind of presidential power they were up against.

At 2:00 A.M. on Tuesday, the president called Walter Reuther in Detroit. He sent him to Atlantic City with a deal. The MFDP would get two seats. They would go to Aaron Henry and Ed King. Henry was chosen because he was chairman of the delegation. King was chosen because he was white and would represent the hope for a desegregated Mississippi. The rest of the MFDP delegation would be treated as "honored guests." As for the regular Mississippi Democrats, those who pledged loyalty to the party's nominee would be seated. At future conventions, no delegation would be seated that did not represent *all* of the people of its state. The Democratic

Supporters of the MFDP kept up an all-night vigil outside the convention hall in an effort to get the MFDP delegation seated.

Party would set up a special committee to help keep that promise.

Reuther explained the deal at an early-morning meeting. He called it a compromise, but in fact it was an order from President Johnson. Aaron Henry, Ed King, and Bob Moses were at the meeting. Martin Luther King and other civil rights leaders were also there.

Fannie Lou Hamer was not there. After the meeting with Humphrey, the MFDP had decided that she was "too unpredictable." She was too independent. However, she was present later that morning when the full delegation met to consider the offer. No deal, the MFDP said.

They would accept nothing short of Congresswoman Green's proposal to seat anyone who would take the loyalty oath.

The credentials committee was about to meet when Joseph Rauh got a call from Reuther. The "compromise" *had* to be accepted by the convention. Rauh knew politics. He understood that Johnson's plan was a victory for the MFDP. It was true that the full delegation would not be seated. However, the MFDP had opened up the party to full participation by African Americans, not just in Mississippi, but in every southern state.

Rauh knew that the MFDP would not see it that way. The delegates had come a long way to be a part of this convention. They believed that they had right on their side. Now they were not even being allowed to choose who would get the two seats. The party had chosen for them: a middle-class black professional and a white man. "Half our delegation is sharecroppers," Rauh told a party official. "Aren't they to be represented? Didn't that ever dawn on you guys?"

The full committee was about to meet. It was going to vote on the compromise *now,* and the subcommittee was urging a "yes" vote. Rauh asked for time to speak to Aaron Henry. He knew that there wasn't time to poll all of the MFDP delegates, but he wanted Henry to give his views. Rauh was shouted down. Everyone was shouting, "Vote! Vote! Vote!" The vote was taken. Rauh was one of eight who voted against the compromise, but 11 votes were needed to block it. It was a done deal.

The MFDP delegation was divided. Some people wanted to accept the compromise and call it a moral victory. Others were bitterly against it. They wanted a floor fight. They wanted an angry demonstration before TV cameras. Many civil rights leaders—such as Whitney Young, Bayard Rustin, and Andrew Young—urged the MFDP to accept. Politics is the art of give-and-take, they explained.

Fannie Lou Hamer didn't know what to do. Leaders she admired were telling her to give up her fight. They told her that the MFDP delegation had made their point, so they could pack up and go home. Home? To what? To Mississippi? To humiliation and fear? What kind of victory was that? What had they gained? Mrs. Hamer respected the SNCC leaders most of all. She asked Ella Baker and Bob Moses what they thought she should do. Moses told her that it was her decision to make.

So she did. Fannie Lou became a voice against the compromise. Who were these people telling them that they had won? *They* hadn't been beaten and shot at in Mississippi, that was clear. She was furious at Aaron Henry and Ed King for agreeing to the compromise. She urged her people to reject the two seats. "We left with nothing, and we'll come home with nothing!" she said.

Other delegates also spoke against the deal. However, as one SNCC worker remembered, it was Fannie Lou Hamer who "more than anybody . . . carried the

Several members of the MFDP gained entrance to the convention using credentials provided by delegates from northern states. They took the empty seats of the departed regular Mississippi delegation, but were finally removed.

delegation. She knew exactly who she was representing and why. She was unbreakable."

The delegation voted to reject the compromise. That evening, they marched to the convention hall, singing "We Shall Overcome." They were going to use their "honored guest" tickets to get in. They found the New Jersey State Police blocking the door. The officers claimed that the fire department had closed the hall because it was too crowded. After a while, they were allowed in.

The convention heard the credentials committee report. There was no debate. Nothing was said about the MFDP's rejection of the compromise. In three minutes, the convention voted to seat the regular Mississippi delegation. The regulars weren't there, however. All but three of them had gone home. They had refused to sign the oath of loyalty to the convention's nominee.

Delegates from other states had offered to let Fannie Lou Hamer and other MFDP delegates take their seats on the floor. Others, including Bob Moses, moved into the empty Mississippi section. Convention business stopped for two hours as guards tried to remove them. They remained standing silently, wearing pictures of the late President Kennedy around their necks.

Several days later, the Freedom Democrats went home to Mississippi. They held a meeting to tell their supporters what had happened. There was no singing.

CHAPTER 8
To Africa...and Back Home

The president wore a long white robe. He looked very much like a leader, Mrs. Hamer thought. He smiled at her. She reached out to shake his hand. Instead, he swept her up in his arms and gave her a big hug.

No one had ever seen Fannie Lou Hamer speechless before. She began to cry. For so long she had tried to meet with the president of her own country. Now Sékou Touré, president of the African nation of Guinea, was receiving her as an honored guest. No, not as a guest. Africa was her home, Touré told her, and its people were her family.

It was September 1964. Freedom Summer was over. The entertainer Harry Belafonte had raised money to take 11 SNCC workers on a trip to Africa. The group decided among themselves who would get to make the trip. Bob Moses and James Forman were among those chosen to go. SNCC activists Julian Bond and John Lewis were picked as well. So was Fannie Lou Hamer.

The land and its colors, the people, and the way they lived were all so different from America, Fannie Lou thought. Yet this continent, Africa, was where she had come from. Her people had been taken from here into slavery. Some of the people she met could be her cousins. She would never know.

The trip opened her eyes in many ways. Fannie Lou had never before seen black people who were in charge of banks or who held important positions in government. In many African nations, blacks had been running their own affairs for years. Still, to a black person born and raised in segregated Mississippi, it seemed strange.

In Africa, members of the SNCC group had a chance to get closer to one another. They made plans for when they got home. They all believed that if blacks in Africa could control entire countries, then blacks in Mississippi would at least be able to register to vote.

The challenge by the Mississippi Freedom Democratic Party at the 1964 Democratic Convention was Fannie Lou Hamer's best-known public act. However, she remained active in the struggle for freedom for the rest of her life.

Bob Moses wanted to show the country that the MFDP was in Mississippi to stay. In the fall of 1964, the party ran candidates for Congress in three districts. The candidates were Victoria Gray, Annie Devine, and Fannie Lou Hamer. The state refused to put their names on the ballot. After the election, the MFDP issued a challenge to Congress. The group wanted the House of Representatives to refuse to seat the five white men who had been elected from Mississippi. Because blacks in the state were prevented from voting, the MFDP argued, the election of the five men was illegal. The MFDP did not expect to win the challenge. It wanted to force members of Congress to take sides. The group hoped this would mean one more step toward justice in Mississippi.

William Ryan, a white Democratic congressman from New York, agreed to make the official challenge. MFDP supporters filled the House gallery when Congress opened its new session on January 4, 1965. When the time came to swear in the members of the House, Ryan rose. "I object to the oath being [given] to the gentlemen from Mississippi," he said. Ryan stated his reasons. He asked all members of the House who agreed to stand with him. The MFDP supporters were delighted to see 70 members of the House stand up.

The five Mississippians had to step aside while the rest of the House was sworn in. The normal procedure then would have been to refer the challenge to a committee and swear in the Mississippians. First, however, Congresswoman Edith Green called for a roll call. Each member would have to declare aloud whether he or she favored seating the five members. There were 276 "aye" votes, but 149 House members voted "nay." The MFDP had not expected such strong support.

It would be months before the House committee would decide the question. During that time, MFDP members argued their case with members of Congress. They also took their message to the people. They spoke at meetings around the country. Fannie Lou Hamer had won national fame at the convention the previous summer. Many groups wanted her to come and speak. However, during most of that year, she was busy in Mississippi. She was supporting a farm workers' strike, and she was caring for her daughter, Dorothy Jean. Mrs. Hamer was about to become a grandmother.

President Johnson had easily won the election the previous November. Most black voters had supported him. Most white southerners had not. Now Johnson was under pressure to take additional action in the area of civil rights. In March 1965, Johnson asked Congress to pass a voting rights bill. It would outlaw poll taxes. More importantly, it would place federal officers in counties where African Americans had been prevented from voting. These officers would supervise registration and elections.

Congress passed the voting rights bill. On August 6, President Johnson signed it into law. On September 13, the House committee met to hear the MFDP challenge. Fannie Lou Hamer was the group's star witness. She told the committee that blacks made up 58 percent of the possible voters in the Second Congressional District where she had been a candidate. That meant that if blacks had been allowed to vote, she might have been elected to Congress. She also pointed out what had happened when federal officers were sent to Leflore County under the new law. In just a few weeks, 3,000 blacks had registered to vote.

The MFDP challenge was defeated. However, Mrs. Hamer had once again forced the government's leaders to make choices. Also, the MFDP had drawn more blacks into the political process. White Mississippi was slowly recognizing that change could not be stopped. That spring, Mrs. Hamer sued Sunflower County officials. She tried to block local elections because blacks were still not being allowed to register. In March 1966, a court ruled in her favor and ordered new elections. It was the first real victory for black voting rights in Mississippi.

The following year, African American candidates were on the ballot in two towns in Sunflower County. They lost on election day, but it would not be too much longer before the voting rights law would begin to take effect. In 1968, 15 blacks were elected to local offices in the state. Some of them ran as MFDP candidates. Others ran as independents. Robert Holmes became the first African American since the Reconstruction period to be seated as a Mississippi state legislator.

That same year, the MFDP again planned to choose delegates to the Democratic National Convention. Only

Mississippi and Alabama were planning to send all-white delegations. The national Democratic Party was making good on its part of the 1964 "compromise." It passed a new rule for its credentials committee to follow. The convention could refuse to seat any delegation that was not chosen with the "full participation" of blacks.

In Mississippi, some blacks and whites wondered how the convention would choose between the all-white regulars and the almost-all-black MFDP. They wanted a delegation that would represent *all* of the people of the state. They formed a new group, the Loyal Democrats of Mississippi. MFDP members were angry. They were the ones who had done the hard work of organizing black Mississippians. Instead of fighting the Loyal Democrats, however, the MFDP agreed to join them. Even so, the two groups did not agree on many issues. In particular, the MFDP felt that the Loyalists did not care enough about the needs of poor farm people. Still, the two groups worked together to build a combined delegation. They would present a united challenge to the party regulars.

The convention met in Chicago. This time, the credentials committee seated the challengers. Among the delegates who represented Mississippi at the convention were Fannie Lou Hamer and Aaron Henry. Another delegate was Charles Evers, the brother of the murdered civil rights leader Medgar Evers.

Four years after being denied a seat in Atlantic City, Fannie Lou Hamer addressed the entire 1968 Democratic convention in Chicago.

Once they were seated, they helped support a challenge delegation from Georgia. It was led by Julian Bond. The one-time SNCC leader was now a state legislator. Like the MFDP in 1964, Bond's group claimed that the regular Georgia delegation did not represent the state's Democrats. African Americans were kept from "full participation" in the state party. It was true that there were six blacks in the regular delegation. However, they had been handpicked by the state's racist governor, Lester Maddox. Fannie Lou Hamer shamed them in a speech. "If they [the Georgia blacks] were in Mississippi, they would know they would not be representing us," she said.

   The challengers were awarded half of Georgia's delegate seats. Many MFDP members would have settled for such a compromise in 1964.

   Four years later, Mrs. Hamer was again a delegate at the 1972 Democratic Convention. Thanks to ten years of effort, Mississippi's delegation had the fullest participation of African Americans of any southern state.

   By then, more than 100 blacks held state or local office in Mississippi. One of them was Charles Evers. He had been elected mayor of the city of Fayette in 1969. By 1989, there were more than 600 African Americans in elective office in the state. One of them was Mike Espy. This son of sharecroppers was elected to Congress from the Second District of Mississippi in 1986.

Voting rights would always be Mrs. Hamer's most important cause, but she was concerned with other matters, as well. Education was particularly important to her. She knew that black people were kept poor and ignorant through second-rate schooling. The Supreme Court had called for equal education in 1954. Years later, however, most African American students still attended segregated schools. Mrs. Hamer supported lawsuits against such two-level school systems in Mississippi. In 1970, she and 104 others filed their own suit against Sunflower County. They won the right to one school system for all county students. They also won protection for the jobs of African American teachers when the schools were combined.

In 1965, the federal government began Project Head Start. This was a preschool program for the children of poor families. In the early 1970s, Mrs. Hamer was involved in a bitter fight over who should control the Head Start program in Sunflower County. One program was run by the county. There was also a grass-roots program organized by the poor people themselves. This group wanted federal money to run its own program separate from the county's.

This was one fight in which Fannie Lou Hamer later regretted getting involved. She was connected with the grass-roots group. Later, she decided that the only way that Head Start could work was as one program. The grass-roots group felt that she had betrayed them. There was a lot of angry talk. Black people in the community were divided. Someone threw a bomb at the Hamer house. Fortunately, it didn't go off. After some time had passed, peace was restored between Mrs. Hamer and her neighbors.

The rights of poor farm people also concerned her. After all, she was one of them. Mississippi farm workers were the lowest-paid workers in the United States. In 1969, their average pay was 95 cents an hour. More and more farm jobs in Mississippi were lost every year, and few farm workers had the education to do anything else.

Land ownership was the answer, Mrs. Hamer believed. There were 31,000 black people in Sunflower County, and only 17 owned any land. In 1969, she started a drive to raise money for Freedom Farm. It would be a farm co-op. Families would own it as a group. They would pay a dollar a month to be members. They would share the work, the food they raised, and any profit they made. Families who couldn't afford a dollar a month could still get fresh vegetables by helping to harvest the crops.

Freedom Farm started on 40 acres. Later, the co-op bought farm machinery and 640 more acres. However, it never did succeed. The families that ran it had no business experience. Some families took food but did no work. The co-op was kept alive through donations. In January 1974, nearly all of the land had to be sold to pay debts and taxes.

The failure of Freedom Farm was one of Fannie Lou Hamer's deepest disappointments. She had been in poor health for years, ever since her beating in Winona. After Freedom Farm failed, she had to be hospitalized, suffering from a nervous breakdown.

From then on, her health only got worse. There were a few moments when some of her old energy returned. She continued to work for voter registration. Now and then she would sing at a rally for poor people's rights. In July 1975, she hosted women from around the world who had been attending an International Women's Year meeting in Mexico.

Most of the time, though, she was alone and in pain. Her older daughter, Dorothy Jean, had died. Her younger daughter, Vergie, had moved away. This woman, who had done so much for people, now had trouble getting anyone to help her. In the spring of 1976, Mrs. Hamer had surgery for breast cancer. It failed to cure her.

That October, the town of Ruleville held a Fannie Lou Hamer Day. Her old friends from the civil rights movement raised money for her medical bills. In a speech, Charles Evers urged people to vote in the upcoming election "to make sure Fannie's work was not in vain."

Fannie Lou Hamer died on March 14, 1977. Andrew Young came to Ruleville to speak at her funeral. When they had first met, he was the director of the SCLC school for citizenship teachers in Georgia. In 1972, he had been elected to Congress. Now, in 1977, he was Ambassador to the United Nations. He had been named to that job by his fellow Georgian, President Jimmy Carter. The votes of black southerners had helped make Carter president—and helped make Young the U.N. ambassador.

Young paid tribute to all of the voting rights activists from the sixties like Mrs. Hamer whose work helped bring about the election of so many blacks years later.

Mrs. Hamer "shook the foundations of this nation," Young told the mourners. "And there was not one of those [black officials] that was not influenced and inspired by the spirit of this one woman."

Acknowledgements

The publisher and the author wish to acknowledge that the following sources were used for background information in the preparation of this biography.

Belfrage, Sally, *Freedom Summer.* Charlottesville, VA: University of Virginia Press, 1990.
Carson, Clayborne, *et. al., The Eyes on the Prize Civil Rights Reader.* New York: Penguin Books, 1991.
Hampton, Henry, and Steve Fayer, *Voices of Freedom.* New York: Bamtam, 1990.
Mills, Kay, *This Little Light of Mine: The Life of Fannie Lou Hamer.* New York: Dutton, 1993.
Van Deburg, William L., *New Day in Babylon.* Chicago: University of Chicago Press, 1992.